D0999771

(A New True Book)

THE FLAG OF THE UNITED STATES

By Dennis B. Fradin

CHILDRENS PRESS ®
CHICAGO

A young boy proudly carries the flag
of the United States of America.

PHOTO CREDITS

Cameramann International, Ltd.—Cover,
4 (bottom right), 21

Journalism Services:
  © Harvey Moshman—24
  © James Quinn—6 (left)

Historical Pictures Service, Chicago—9 (left), 13,
14, 17 (left), 19, 22 (left), 33, 39

© Norma Morrison—2, 7, 37, 45 (right)

NASA—4 (bottom left), 42

Nawrocki Stock Photo:
  © Rui Coutinho—24 (right)
  © Richard Clement—4 (top)
  © Robert Lightfoot III—45 (left)

Photri—6 (right), 17 (right), 20, 32 (2 photos),
35 (right), 44 (2 photos)

© H. Armstrong Roberts—27, 35 (left)

Root Resources:
  © MacDonald Photography—41

Courtesy Flag Research Center, Winchester,
Massachusetts: —9 (right), 11, 22 (left), 29, 31

Cover: A circle of U.S. flags surrounds the
Washington Monument in Washington, D.C.

Library of Congress Cataloging-in-Publication Data

Fradin, Dennis B.
  The flag of the United States / by Dennis B. Fradin
    p.   cm. — (A new true book)
  Includes index.
  Summary: Traces the history of the American flag,
explains why the flag is an important symbol of our
country, and illustrates ways people observe and care
for the flag.
  ISBN 0-516-01158-8
  1. Flags—United States—History—Juvenile
literature. [1. Flags—History.] I. Title.
CR113.F83   1988   88-15436
929.9'2—dc19   CIP
                                            AC

Childrens Press®, Chicago
Copyright ©1988 by Regensteiner Publishing Enterprises, Inc.
All rights reserved. Published simultaneously in Canada.
Printed in the United States of America.
1 2 3 4 5 6 7 8 9 10 R 98 97 96 95 94 93 92 91 90 89 88

TABLE OF CONTENTS

Flags are displayed outside public buildings and on the uniforms of people who work for the government.

THE FLAG STANDS FOR THE COUNTRY

The red, white, and blue United States flag can be seen in many places. The flag flies over public buildings. Children say the Pledge of Allegiance at school. Some government workers wear flag patches on their uniforms. People sing "The Star-Spangled Banner" to the flag at many sporting events.

Businesses and homes often fly the American flag
to express their love for the United States.

Some people even fly the
flag over their homes.
A flag is a piece of
cloth with great meaning. A
country's flag is a symbol
of the country. It stands
for the country and its

6

people. When people say
the Pledge of Allegiance,
they are promising to be
loyal to the flag and their
country. When they sing
"The Star-Spangled
Banner," they are
expressing love for the
United States of America.

FLAGS IN EARLIER TIMES

The ancient Egyptians
are thought to have made
the first flags. That was
about 6,000 years ago.
Their flags were usually
carved wooden emblems
mounted on poles. No
single flag stood for all of
Egypt. Different parts of
Egypt had their own flags.

Denmark was one of the
first countries to have a

The first Egyptian flags (left) were carved wooden symbols mounted on poles. The flag of Denmark (above) was designed in 1219.

national flag. In the year 1219 Denmark's King Valdemar is said to have seen a white cross in the red sky. A white cross on red has been Denmark's flag ever since.

Other nations soon had their own flags, too.

England had a flag by the late 1200s. It was a red cross on a white field. Scotland had a flag about 100 years later. It was a white cross shaped like an X on a blue field.

In 1603 England and Scotland joined under one king. Three years later, England's and Scotland's flags were joined to make a new flag. It was red, white, and blue. It was called the *Union Jack*.

St. George's flag (above left) of England was combined with St. Andrew's flag (left) of Scotland to make a new flag (above). This was the original Union Jack designed in 1606, three years after England and Scotland were joined under one ruler.

This was the new flag of Great Britain.

The red, white, and blue colors of the Union Jack later were used in the American flag. There was reason for this. From 1607 to 1776, Britain ruled the eastern coast of America.

THE YEARS OF BRITISH RULE

In 1607 Great Britain founded its first permanent American colony. This was the Virginia Colony. Britain later ruled twelve more colonies in what is now the United States. The Union Jack flew over the thirteen American colonies.

The Stamp Act made the citizens of Boston angry with the British government.

For many years Americans were happy with British rule. But then in the 1760s and 1770s Britain tried to make them pay taxes. The Americans thought this was unfair.

Painting showing the Battle of Bunker Hill

In 1775 the Americans began fighting a war against Britain. But they did not yet want to break free of the mother country. They just wanted fairer treatment.

THE FIRST UNITED STATES FLAG

Soon after the war began in 1775, Americans wanted their own flag. American leaders talked it over. They decided that their flag should look like the Union Jack. Yet it had to be different enough to show that it was the flag of the thirteen colonies.

They created a new flag in late 1775. It had a small

Union Jack in one corner.
But it also had seven
red and six white stripes.
The thirteen stripes stood
for the thirteen colonies.
This flag was called the
Continental Colors.

By 1776 Americans
wanted to have their own
country. On July 4, 1776,
American leaders approved
the Declaration of
Independence. This paper
said that the United States
was free of Britain.

A copy of the
Declaration of
Independence (left),
and the Continental
Colors (above)

The Continental Colors
was still being used at the
time. Thus it became the
first United States flag.

THE STARS AND STRIPES

Americans soon felt that they should have a new flag. They had said they were free and independent. And they were fighting the Revolutionary War to win that freedom. Why should they have a flag that looked so much like Britain's?

The country did get a new flag—the Stars and Stripes. Exactly when and

Painting shows Betsy Ross (standing) and her helpers making the first American flag.

how this happened is not known. And nobody knows who should get the credit.

Some say that Betsy Ross made the first American flag that had stars and stripes. Betsy Ross lived in Philadelphia.

She sewed clothes and other items, including flags.

According to one story, George Washington and two other men visited Betsy Ross in the summer of 1776. This was about when the Declaration of Independence was

George Washington, George Ross (standing), and Robert Morris receive the first American flag from Betsy Ross.

A copy of the flag Betsy Ross made hangs outside her home in Philadelphia, Pennsylvania.

approved. The three men asked Betsy to make a new United States flag. They gave her an idea of what they wanted, but Betsy had some ideas of her own. She then made

Some historians say that Francis Hopkinson (left) designed the Stars and Stripes (right).

the first flag with stars and stripes, but this has not been proved.

There is another story about how the Stars and Stripes came to be. According to this one, Francis Hopkinson designed it. He was a New Jersey signer of the Declaration of Independence.

Hopkinson was also a judge, author, and songwriter.

Did Betsy Ross or Francis Hopkinson create the first Stars and Stripes? Or did someone else do it? We do not know. But we do know that on June 14, 1777, the United States passed a law. The U.S. flag was to have thirteen stars and thirteen stripes. The stars and stripes stood for the thirteen states.

June 14—when the Stars

and Stripes became the
official U.S. flag—became
a special day. It is called
Flag Day. Most people
who own American flags
fly them on Flag Day. But
of course the American
flag now has more than
thirteen stars!

WHAT TO DO ABOUT NEW STATES?

The thirteen stars and thirteen stripes were fine— as long as the country had thirteen states. But in 1791 Vermont became the fourteenth state. In 1792 Kentucky became the fifteenth state. They wanted to be honored on the flag, too.

In 1794 Congress decided to change the

flag. By 1795 the new one was ready. It had fifteen stripes and fifteen stars to honor the fifteen states. This flag was up-to-date for just a short time. In 1796 Tennessee became the sixteenth state. Then came Ohio in 1803, Louisiana in 1812, Indiana in 1816, and Mississippi in 1817.

Mississippi was the twentieth state. Yet by the end of 1817 the United States was still using the

The flag with fifteen stripes and fifteen stars was raised over Fort Mifflin, an historic site in Pennsylvania.

flag with fifteen stripes and fifteen stars.

U.S. lawmakers had a problem. They could not add a stripe and a star for each new state. What if one day the country had forty states, or even fifty?

With all those stars and stripes, the flag would be very crowded.

In 1818 the United States made a new law. The U.S. flag would always have thirteen stripes to honor the first thirteen states. But a star would be added for each new state.

The flag kept changing as more states joined the country. By 1848 the flag had thirty stars. But no rule told how the stars should be placed. For

The 26-star flag (above left), the 30-star flag (above), and the 36-star flag (left). Stars were added as new states joined the United States of America.

example, after Nevada became a state in 1864, the flag had 36 stars. On some flags they were placed in six rows of six stars each. On others the 36 stars were arranged to make one big star.

The placement of the stars was decided in 1912, when New Mexico and Arizona became the 47th and 48th states. President William Howard Taft said that the stars on all U.S. flags should be placed the same way. The 48 stars should be in six rows of eight stars each.

The flag of 1912 lasted the longest of any U.S. flag so far. It was used until 1959, when Alaska became the 49th state.

The 48-star flag (above left), the 49-star flag (center), and the 50-star flag (above right). Since 1959 no new states have joined the Union and no new stars have been added to the U.S. flag.

But the 49-star flag (seven rows of seven stars) lasted for just a short while. Later in 1959 Hawaii became the fiftieth state. A new flag was designed. Still in use, the 50-star flag has five rows with six stars each and four rows with five stars each.

Huge machines (above) are used
to cut out the stars, which are
then sewed by machine onto the flag.

One day new states may
join the United States. If
that happens, more stars
will be added to the flag.
Can you think of ways to
arrange a 51-star flag? Or
a 52-star flag?

"THE STAR-SPANGLED BANNER"

Francis Scott Key

The special song about the United States flag is called "The Star-Spangled Banner." It is the national anthem, or official song, of the United States of America.

Francis Scott Key of Maryland wrote "The

Star-Spangled Banner" in 1814. The United States was then fighting another war against Great Britain. On a September night in 1814 the British bombed Fort McHenry, which guarded Baltimore, Maryland. They hoped to take the fort and then burn Baltimore.

The British bombed Fort McHenry all night. Francis Scott Key watched from a nearby boat as the bombs burst in the air. But he

THE STAR-SPANGLED BANNER

Painting (above) shows Francis Scott Key watching the battle for Fort McHenry.

was not sure what was happening. Then, by the dawn's early light, he saw something thrilling. The United States flag was still there! The British had not

35

taken Fort McHenry. They would not take Baltimore.

Francis Scott Key was so happy that he wrote a poem. "Oh! say, can you see, by the dawn's early light," it began. It went on for many more lines. The poem was soon set to music. "The Star-Spangled Banner" became very popular. In 1931 the U.S. Congress named it the national anthem.

THE PLEDGE
TO THE FLAG

People also say some special words to the flag. These words are called the Pledge of Allegiance. The pledge is a promise of loyalty to the country.

I pledge allegiance to the flag of the United States of America and to the Republic for which it stands, one Nation under God, indivisible, with liberty and justice for all.

The pledge was written by another man named Francis. He was Francis Bellamy of Boston, Massachusetts. Bellamy wrote the pledge in 1892. In 1942 Congress made the pledge an official vow of loyalty to the United States. In 1954 the words "under God" were added.

SOME GREAT MOMENTS FOR THE FLAG

The United States flag has had many great moments. One came during the Revolutionary War. In 1777 navy hero John Paul Jones flew the Stars and Stripes

The *Ranger* (right) is believed to be one of the first ships to fly the Stars and Stripes in battle.

over the *Ranger*. This was the first time the American flag flew over a warship.

Another great moment came during World War II. In 1945 the United States and Japan fought for the island called Iwo Jima. The Americans finally won it. A photo was taken of American soldiers raising the flag on Iwo Jima.

The flag has had great moments in peacetime, too. In 1909 the explorer

This statue in Arlington National Cemetery honors the men who fought on Iwo Jima during World War II. It was modeled after a famous photograph.

Robert E. Peary reached the North Pole with his men. To show that Americans had reached the pole first, they planted the American flag.

Many people thought the

In 1969 the U.S. flag was planted on the moon.

North Pole was the most
remote place the flag
would fly. But in 1969 the
U.S. astronauts landed on
the moon. They planted
the American flag on the
moon—240,000 miles
from home.

SPECIAL DAYS
AND SPECIAL CARE

The American flag has nicknames. People call it the "Stars and Stripes," the "Star-Spangled Banner," "Old Glory," or "the Red, White, and Blue."

There are certain days when Americans are urged to fly their flags. Those special days are:

Abraham Lincoln's Birthday
George Washington's Birthday
the Fourth of July

Memorial Day
Flag Day
Veterans Day

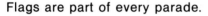
Flags are part of every parade.

There are also special
rules for caring for the
flag. On school days it
should be flown in or near
each school. The flag
should not be flown
outside in bad weather. It
should not be used for

advertising. It should not
touch the ground. It should
be flown at voting places
on election days.

The flag is an important
symbol of the country.
That is why it should be
treated with love and care.

WORDS YOU SHOULD KNOW

ancient(AIN • shint) — very, very old

astronauts(AST • ro • nawts) — space explorers

colony(KAHL • uh • nee) — a settlement built by a country beyond its borders

Continental Colors(kahn • tih • NEN • tul KUL • erz) — the first U.S. flag

Declaration of Independence(deck • luh • RAY • shun UV in • dih • PEN • dence) — the paper which said that the American colonies were breaking free of Britain in 1776

flag(FLAG) — a piece of cloth that a country uses as a symbol

Flag Day(FLAG DAY) — June 14, the day the Stars and Stripes was adopted in 1777

national anthem(NASH • uh • nu! AN • thum) — a country's official song

Old Glory(OLD GLORE • ree) — a nickname for the U.S. flag

Pledge of Allegiance(PLEJ UV uh • LEE • jance) — a promise of loyalty to the United States; also called the Pledge to the Flag

Revolutionary War(rev • uh • LOO • shun • airy WAHR) — the war the United States fought to free itself from Britain

Stars and Stripes(STAHRZ AND STRYPES) — a nickname for the U.S. flag

"The Star-Spangled Banner"(STAHR SPANG • ild BAN • ner) — the national anthem of the United States of America

symbol(SIM • bul) — something that reminds people of something else; the American flag is a symbol of the United States

INDEX

About the Author

Dennis Fradin attended Northwestern University on a partial creative scholarship and graduated in 1967. His previous books include the Young People's Stories of Our States series for Childrens Press and Bad Luck Tony *for Prentice-Hall. In the True book series Dennis has written about astronomy, farming, comets, archaeology, movies, space colonies, the space lab, explorers, and pioneers. He is married and the father of three children.*